The Shape of Ukraine

Poems inspired by the war

By Stephen Gospage

GW01057523

ISBN: 978-1-917425-02-5

Stephen Gospage, a writer of poetry and short stories, was born in London in 1953 and spent most of his working life in Brussels. Now retired, he lives in Belgium, close to Waterloo. He has dual British and Belgian nationality and is proud to call himself a citizen of Europe. Several of his poems have appeared in the *New European* newspaper. He has written many poems on the Ukraine war and is a regular contributor to the *Write Out Loud* poetry blog. He would like to thank all those involved with *Write Out Loud* for their support and encouragement.

Three of his poems have appeared in '*Poems for Ukraine*', an anthology published in July 2022 by Poetry Performance.

Introduction

I started writing poems about Russia's invasion of Ukraine at the beginning of the conflict in February 2022. The poems are the reflections of an outsider and keen (though often shocked and outraged) observer who made several visits to Kyiv during the 1990s.

War stirs up different and terrible emotions. On the most basic level, it is awful. Soldiers and civilians are killed, towns and cities destroyed, and many people are forced to flee. Conflict is an aberration; there should never be a situation in which human beings are allowed to maim and murder each other.

I am never going to be a cheerleader for war. The pity and the pointlessness of it repels me. A part of me wants the fighting to stop so that no one else dies and the millions of refugees are able to return. In some respects, I find it unfortunate that democratic countries in the West are having to send lethal weapons to help perpetuate the carnage.

However, first and foremost, I respect Ukraine's right to defend itself and salute the bravery of its people, particularly the civilians, who have often undergone unimaginable suffering. I do not want to see naked aggression rewarded; whatever one thinks of Ukraine's bid for EU membership, it has the right to see its future in Europe if it so chooses. It is, in the end, essential that the western world stands up to bullying, and to all the misinformation that goes with it.

At the time of writing, near the end of 2022, there is no end in sight. Although Ukraine has retaken some occupied territory, Russia's bombardment of critical infrastructure and its annexation of most of East Ukraine, through a series of sham referendums, has potentially taken the conflict into new and even more dangerous areas. The use of nuclear weapons, something previously unthinkable, is now talked about as a serious option. There is even talk of 'Ukraine fatigue' among Western officials and citizens who are preoccupied with the high energy prices and other costs which have resulted from the war. And so, regretfully in some ways, I continue to write poetry which attempts to reflect the concerns and contradictions expressed above.

I have selected the following forty poems from my output. They are all relatively short and are presented in the order that I wrote them. The first, 'Musée des Beaux-Arts, March 2022' was written just after the war started; the last, 'Refugee', dates from early November. The title poem was written in mid-July.

Most of these poems have been shared on the *Write Out Loud* poetry website and three of them: 'Staged Event', 'Missile' and 'Carnival' have appeared in '*Poems for Ukraine',* an anthology published in July 2022 by Poetry Performance.

All proceeds from this book will go to charities assisting the Ukrainian people.

Contents

Title	Page

Musée des Beaux-Arts, March 2022

*(Inspired by a visit to Brussels' Fine Arts Museum
to see Bruegel's The Fall of Icarus, which W.H.
Auden referred to in his 1939 poem 'Musée des
Beaux Arts'.)*

It's hard to believe that Auden stood here
And stared while Europe teetered on the brink.
The tiny Icarus, unseen, ignored,
By locals who have better things to do,
Drops down beneath the weight of melted wings.
But this and other paintings have survived,
Unchanged for centuries through conflicts, plagues,
Achievements and disasters, rattling past
Beyond these walls. They are the permanent.
Later, I exit onto the street. The sun,
With springtime vigour, warms up passers-by.
War seems far away; peace seems further still.

A Time to Write

It seems a waste of time to write
While shots ring out
And bombs and missiles fall,
While populations flee
And others have their backs against the wall,
While bullies swagger round the land
And choose which puppets to install,
It seems a waste of time to write.

No! This is what the strongmen want:
Put down your pen and call it a day.
They seek monopolies on words,
Where peace means war
And truth means lies
So long as it is someone else
Who stands before a tank and dies.

First trip to Kyiv, June 1996

An early morning flight from Vienna,
The plane stuffed with consultants in their suits;
Rugby scrums for visas on arrival.
Hotel post-Soviet, with quirky charm:
'Three hundred dollars. You pay in cash. Now!'
On each floor women at desks dole out keys
And watch cartoons on cinema-sized screens.
No one can close the window in my room.
The metro staircase seems to reach Earth's core.
No shooting or bombing of the market,
Where people sell their dreams. The churches are
Glorious. In spite of what is to come,
One feels there is a future for this place,
A destiny. Back at base, the phone rings:
'Hi. You like beautiful Russian lady?'
That is one call you would not get today.

The President

The President roared, The President roared:
'I have so much power, yet I am bored.'

The President thought, The President thought:
'What can I do for today's bit of sport?'

The President said, The President said:
'Bring me that man and I'll chop off his head.'

The President cried, The President cried:
'Now I shed tears for the man who just died.'

The President lied.

Carnival

In time of war, things fit to you tightly:
No bagginess, no slack, no surplus inch.
War exposes us as human beings,
And makes us face ourselves for what we are.
The carnival starts; you put on your mask
And run to meet your girl. Later, waking,
You hear a distant cry from your old friend,
Pleading for your help through the gas and mud.
But you are too warm; she is beside you,
Keen as a whip. The cry melts to silence.
Next day comes the knock. Sad entertainers
Dance quietly around the carousel.
In the mirror, you see your guilty grin
Fall down flat, to where nobody can hear.

Staged Event

(Russian spokesmen refer to the discovery of civilian bodies in Bucha as a 'Staged Event')

It wasn't that complicated,
But it had to be authentic.
No point in actors playing dead.
Think about it! They'll sneeze or twitch
As the cameras start rolling
And give the whole damn game away.
Luckily, we had true patriots,
Prepared to sacrifice their lives,
Ready to jump in plastic bags
And take a bullet in the head.
Thousands were queueing round the block,
Cheered on by happy families.
Who else would perform such a stunt?
Enemies are such nice people.

'Grieving Ukrainian Mother' (as seen on TV)

(TV channels describe a witness as a 'Grieving Ukrainian Mother')

The caption caught my eye with morning tea;
Tearful in woe, she loomed large on the screen.
The opened plastic bag revealed her son;
Her heartbreak and distress were hard to bear.
The brother held her in a sad caress;
Distraught, they parried questions from the press.

And I was torn. Should this not be discreet,
This tragedy, and not for public view?
Then someone else, a man, saw his friend, dead,
And turned away and ran with head in hands.
The image closed, as though in hot pursuit.
Could they be spared the clutches of this brute?

Sadly, the answer in the end is no.
We see this truth, though inconsiderate,
And understand and do what must be done.
If not, we just rely on feeds of news
And pundits throwing numbers everywhere,
But not the reason why some fight, or care.

Graves

(Two Russian soldiers are tried for murdering civilians).

Could you forgive the people who did this?
For those removed, in some comfortable spot,
It may sound like a question of process.
But, first and foremost, our grieving heart
Must come to terms with unrepentant brutes,
Sneering at the glory of their capture.
Stripped of our rage and experience,
Our mind, our trained intelligence, may think:
A necessary step to finding peace,
To cleansing our heads and starting anew.
But part, reacting, will choose to rebel
And wish the swine to squirm and melt away.
Wounds, as in the graves, fester and remain.

Missile

I popped out to the shops to buy some bread;
When I returned my family were dead.
A missile had destroyed our neighbourhood;
From this time onwards, nothing will be good.
I cannot understand these men of war;
I cannot comprehend what this is for.
We had no quarrel with our former friends;
How can these means advance their twisted ends?
Were they at war, my children and my wife?
They wished for no more than to live their life.
I search among the debris for a sign
Of those whose being intertwined with mine.
As I withdraw beneath the cindered sky,
The hammer in my mind repeats: Why? Why?

Apology

I'm sorry your husband bought it.
I'm sorry we killed your son,
And your daughter, and your cat,
And that we blew up your house,
And raped your best friend next door,
And made you flee the country.
But, you see, we had no choice;
We must protect and free you
From Nazis, degenerates,
NATO, Zelensky, the EU, yourselves,
From anyone, except us.
We know what you people like.
Please take this apology
In the spirit intended.

Death of a Gardener

(There is apparently serious talk of Russia deploying nuclear weapons)

You may encounter his remains, they say,
Preserved in ashes, at the break of day.
A handsome form, a scarecrow for our time,
Abandoned at this place of greatest crime.
He laboured when they launched the 'Big Event',
A mass elimination their intent.
Though thousands were consumed, his shape
survived;
His cheery face and smile may be long gone,
But early risers see him wield his hoe.
Tactical? Strategic? How could he know?

Lenin

(A statue of Lenin goes up in an occupied Ukrainian town)

I thought he would be giving us a wave,
But no. An old gent, looking quite cheesed off.
As an individual, he had good points,
But I don't want his statue in this town.
He has too much baggage; I'm short on tact.
Anyway, we do not need more clutter.
These damned edifices are everywhere:
Footballers, dogs, forgotten men in wigs.
In some spots you can hardly move for them.
The one in our square seemed a decent sort:
An artist, and a patriot to boot.
No prizes for guessing where he has gone.
They said they had to fill the space, but then
They said they were bringing us freedom, so…

Anger Management

(The Victory Day parade in Moscow, 9 May 2022)

We should not yield to anger,
Nor trespass upon kindness.
There are other ways to staunch the boiling blood.
The sight of yesterday's Victory parade,
With its wind-up, flat-pack military,
Its gross salutes and guns and strut,
Its little man made out of wax,
Talking for ages through his nut,
Made me grimace at the waste
And at the tragic, pointless load
Of fresh-dead bodies, laid in haste
On some unprized suburban road.
In response, I squirmed at every stomp
And laughed, yes laughed, at all the pomp.

Future Prospects

You wake again in dawn's reluctant light;
The neighbour's wife and youngster have both fled.
He shivers as he clings hold of his gun
And, unrefreshed, falls on his lonely bed.

Looking back, war can be a lucky break.
Men who once cleaned up a factory floor,
When it is over, build a better life;
At present, it's a terrifying chore

Of trembling hands, impending sense of doom.
Intruders sharpen blades and mass nearby,
The smoke of bombs and shells hangs in the air,
The fear of what's to come makes mouths run dry.

The waiting can be viewed as breathing space;
We know this nightmare must come to an end.
Yet the uncertain, with its vice-like grasp,
Makes future prospects hard to apprehend.

War Poems

I never wrote a poem about war;
I would find a thousand reasons not to.
But then I see what's happening out there
And, sadly, I believe that I have got to.

All war seemed safely abstract and remote,
But now the horror flickers on my screen.
Guilt of absence and my indignation
Seep down into the day's humdrum routine.

So picking up my pen is one small way
To make a tiny speck of difference,
To roll a rough-edged stone towards the pond
And come down from my smug, indulgent fence.

City Tour

Good afternoon, you've come from far and wide;
In Mariupol, I shall be your guide.
Do not believe the lying foreign press,
Who will pretend this place is one big mess.
Just look at the improvements we have made:
All that extra space, if a bit less shade.
(And any minor damage has been done
By outside agents who have cut and run).
You see that souvenir shop with its flags?
Our leader's face adorns its plastic bags.
Once there was a school beneath this rubble,
Till our brave boys rooted out the trouble.
All those busloads going on vacation,
Are no longer part of this great nation.
Whichever way you look, the future's bright,
And soon we may have power for the light.

Landmines

I wonder if those who lay the mines down
Stay put and wait for victims to approach,
Or, with a surreptitious grin, retreat.
As for the victims, no imagining
The horror of their plight will bring them back.
The miner and mined have done their duty.
In moral terms, they seem so far apart:
One bad, one innocent. But consider.
They are both under orders not to think:
Playthings, creations of puppet masters.
Their actions, predetermined, are foretold.
Bad is not evil, innocence not good.
In war, who notices? All play a role;
Each slouching around, hoping it will end.

Splendid Youth

The war is sucking up our splendid youth.
They're racing to the front; they won't come back.
Each town and village starts to empty out,
As friends and classmates go on the attack.
They're fighting for our dignity and state
Of freedom and of happiness pursued,
But consequences, each one plainly knows,
Could be unmentionably vile and rude.
In these now quiet streets the young once dreamt
And plotted better worlds, from dawn to dusk.
Those who return will never be the same;
If frames are sound, their minds will be a husk.
The greater good may warrant sacrifice,
But war's destroyed illusions are not nice.

Dying in Ukraine

They're dying every minute in Ukraine.
They die up at the front and in the towns,
Cheered on by generals and circus clowns
Who push the envelope to entertain
With their own brand of tragedy and pain.

They're dying every minute in Ukraine.
Lives may be swapped for twenty feet of land,
Transactions nobody can understand,
Fought out in summer heat or pouring rain.
It happened once; it's happening again.

They're dying every minute in Ukraine.
Limp bodies dangle from the burning blocks,
While top brass busily turn back the clocks.
Grim relatives won't grumble or complain,
When told their loss is everybody's gain.

They're dying every minute in Ukraine.
They're lying, buried pointlessly beneath
A shallow pretext, lying through its teeth.
The rich stay clear. The poor, who still remain,
Send postcards to remind us of those slain.

Trollies in Kremenchuk

*(In June 2022, a shopping centre in Kremenchuk is
hit Russian missiles)*

I curse the bloody things sometimes.
Last Monday at the Shopping Mall
I grabbed one but a wheel was jammed.
The next one veered off to the right
And the last trolley in the row
Simply collapsed before my eyes.
I went outside to the car park
And spotted a shiny model
In the far corner. Just the job,
I thought, and marched off to claim it.
Light and mobile, it was perfect.

At that moment, the missile fell;
Blown in the air, I was all right.
Unlike many, including some
Who made do with the duff trollies.
Perhaps I am too demanding.

They say life is a lottery,
But one man is off his trolley.

Fancy Names

Let's consider this, just for a moment:
Hundreds are slaughtered in attacks on schools,
On apartment blocks, or shopping centres.
Yet still we call it by fancy names: War.
Special Military Operation.
We hand out medals, salute the inane,
And march up and down wearing silly clothes.
If I sent bombs towards civilians,
I should go down as a mass murderer;
But in this mad world, I am a hero,
Doused with honours and brazenly adored.
Perhaps that's why they are gagging for war;
It's one big turn-on for the drooling crowds,
Who cheer the brave boys home, and who pretend
Their evil is scrubbed out by fancy names.

The Shape of Ukraine

(20% of Ukraine's territory has been occupied).

Though every nation's shape must be unique,
The outline of Ukraine attracts our gaze.
A sense of the vulnerable protrudes
From this quiet space, once so short on hate.
This is where fear comes in; borders store
Culture, landscape, language and traditions,
Encircling the rich plains of history.
More than that, they preserve our memories,
Of sunny dreams, glistening on water.
And yet, in their simplest form, they are lines,
Drawn casually on our map of movements.
They can be crossed, ignored, even laughed at,
And no one will care unless it suits them.
Territory, even counted in the abstract,
Is all we have and is all that matters.
Today, it is our shape that we defend.

Innocents

(On 21 July 2022, it was reported that 15,000 Russians have died in Ukraine and 45,000 have been wounded).

Fifteen thousand Russians dead in Ukraine;
Innocents, for the most part, made guilty
By the vicious vanity of old men,
Using the war like a wild young lover,
To prove they can do it, still get it up.
In their pointless, far-off rumpus, blood spills
As one hundred per day give up the ghost:
Bombed, blasted, burned, shot, all variations
On a path to death. Strewn haphazardly,
Each leave families, multiplying grief.
Locals bury some bodies, while the rest
Are casually bagged, or not seen again.

Three times as many are wounded, not dead;
But that's just a detail, as someone said.

Tanks

Through the spectral quiet
Of this deserted place,
The tanks go rolling by
In their odd little race.

It's hardly a surprise
That they proceed so fast;
There's nothing here to see,
Since that almighty blast.

So, as they disappear
Along the dusty road,
The silence will renew
Its dark, despondent load.

'Write Something'

*(Ukrainian amputees in rehabilitation express a
wish to get back to the front).*

Late one evening, not doing much,
I glimpse the latest news on screen.
Soldiers from Ukraine, dismembered
At the front, battle to insert
The cold stumps of their missing legs
Into new replacement hollows:
Each faltering step agony,
Their cries the rage of raw courage.
All hanker to re-join the fight
And kick the cheap destroyer out.
Anger swells, somewhere. They should be
Fathers, Husbands, Sons, not victims
Of wartime's clucking cowardice.
I stir and scribble down a note:
'Write Something'. But what can one write?
Who sleeps soundly in their skin now?

Afternoon Stroll

(A collection of captured, mostly burned-out,
Russian tanks is displayed in Kyiv in August 2022.)

We strolled down the streets of Kyiv
One balmy August afternoon,
Past burned-out skeletons of tanks,
Which might as well live on the moon.

We understand this rough display,
To boost a noble people's mood,
But battles rage not far away,
Where wrecks like this are caked in blood.

Conflict is a harsh performance;
You enemy is marked as bad.
But truth, uncomfortable, still looms;
All war is desperate and sad.

We should feel pity for these tanks,
Ridiculous though that may seem.
Their universe is bolted on;
Those trapped inside can only scream.

The Big Men

The Big Men limber up for war,
Showing off their guns and rockets;
The Big Men strut around the town,
Looted cash stuffed in their pockets.

The Big Men are toning muscles,
To beat their captives into shape;
The Big Men snigger at reports
Of instances of wartime rape.

The Big Men hide behind the lines,
To dodge the other side's attack;
The Big Men's pastime is to shoot
Unarmed citizens in the back.

The Big Men terrorise the place,
They blow up hospitals and schools;
The Big Men shift the blame for deaths,
And try to take the world for fools.

The Big Men crash and fall to earth,
As even Big Men one day must,
And at this moment they will learn
They are no bigger than the dust.

Izium

(In September 2022, mass graves are discovered as the Ukrainian army retakes the town of Izium. Many of the bodies are civilians and some show signs of torture.)

I knew this one. In different times
She could have led so many lives:
Doctor, artist, mother, teacher,
One of a gang of merry wives.

A guess, of course. She was so young,
And now is hauled out of this pit.
Laid out for ever in a shroud;
Deprived of all her charm and wit.

This place concealed a tragic tale;
A savage tumult oozing waste.
Like her, each one had much to give,
But virtue has long been displaced.

With forks and spades we have exposed
An evil still hard to believe.
Those disinterred now fill out hearts;
In spite of anger, we shall grieve.

Referendum

(Russia conducts sham referendums in four regions of East Ukraine in 2022, as a prelude to their annexation).

What should be a simple counting of heads
Is here a result buried with the bones,
Near to the fenced-off railway sheds.

For freedom's optimistic tidings
Are out of fashion in these parts,
Like wagons mothballed in the sidings.

In place of a future based on trust,
The disused tracks will soon become
A monument to power's naked lust.

This will not be the first time or the last
That memory, with sorrow, fades to sleep
And human failings cower in the past.

Small Print

(Russia 'officially' annexes the four regions on 30 September 2022.)

It's the rifle-butt nature of all this:
Sit down, shut up, sign here, do as you're told.
We talk about land grabs, but this is, well,
An extortion, of dignity and heart.
There's a bash for the scammers in the North,
And jobs for the boys. Lots of them, no doubt.
Imagine this: 'Yes, I'd love to be ruled
By the people who blew this place to bits
And killed or maimed our friends and family.'
'Certainly, sir. Bend down, and I will kick
Your backside halfway down the road for fun.'
Surprised? 'Remember those heavies, touting
With the clipboard? It was all written down.
Hard luck, mate. You should have read the small
print.'

Bastards

Revving up, it seemed a bit of a blast.
We crossed the border, waved, and cried 'At last!'
To civilise this country with no name
Appeared to be a fine and worthy aim.

Though no one seemed that thrilled to see us there,
We pressed ahead without a doubt or care.
Soon Kiev was in range of our attack…
And then the bastards started fighting back!

Apartment Block

I didn't deserve the love that you gave:
I didn't deserve your extinguished heart.
I wish I had been the one to behave
That last time before fate tore us apart.

As one young child is pulled from the rubble,
I realise that you were crushed beneath.
Another search is not worth the trouble;
I'll find a still spot to lay down my wreath.

I hear the sirens and look to the sky,
As missiles flatten today's dreams and lives.
Faced with this slaughter, I ask myself why
We live in a world where such murder thrives.

When you last saw me, I'd travelled all night
And drank too much with my mates on the train.
I was not that nice, if I recall right;
You never wanted to see me again.

And now here I am, and you are not here;
It's hard to explain how that makes me feel.
In all my turmoil of grief and of fear,
I now understand what this war can steal.

Revenge

It's strange how we view war from far away.
Distance lends itself to rage and anger,
To dollops of easy indignation,
Fuelled by being powerless, I suppose.
For those on the spot, it's the practical,
The workaday, which occupies the mind:
Filling in the forms, feeding survivors,
Visiting hospital, booking the hearse.
The task of clearing out dead neighbours' homes
Damps down the anger. At least for a while,
Because it remains: circling, festering,
Nagging at your conscience, and competing
With the grief and numbness of your mourning.
One day, its revenge will be terrible.

The Pity

The pity and the painlessness of war;
Here pointlessness and valour meld as one.
The office worker, finishing her shift,
Believes it safe to cross the peppered road
Just one more time. It turns out not to be,
But the act, with much of her life unlived,
Is quick, with no time for regrets or shame.
Her grandfather, in his basement, with shells
Just missing left and right, says to himself,
'I've had a good, long life. Please make it fast.'
The youth, freshly armed, understands nothing,
Yet knows the paradox of coming fate.
He celebrates the prospect of no pain,
Yet feels, lurking in his heart, the pity.

Brass Monkeys (Winter in Ukraine)

*(I made two winter visits to Ukraine in the late
1990s).*

That's what I thought, arriving in Kyiv.
It was December, and minus fifteen.
'This is nothing,' said the driver. It felt
Like something. Hat, gloves and scarf were no use.
The hotel was marvellously porous,
Rooms glacial, the restaurant shivered
Behind flapping Perspex windows. The wind
Reached all protected parts. The next morning,
To the lecture. Everyone double-wrapped,
But I gave my speech in shirtsleeves and tie
And blew on my hands to stave off frostbite.
Smart ones kept vodka in their office drawer.
Of course, this is but flippant anecdote;
Real winter will grab many by the throat.

Foot Soldiers

Just like the bodies, plucked and sacrificed
In dirty factories and down in mines,
Like frightened masses, banished to the dark,
Or the timebound terror of the trenches,
Here come the foot soldiers, their destinies
Already marked. Convenient agents
In the hands of the men who know better.
It was ever thus. Some are dead, others
Beyond hope, the rest numbered and dated.
Now 'Why did they go, did they understand?'
Resonates louder than it ever has.
And what if some did? Does that improve things?
There is such a thing as futility;
It's playing every day, on phones, TV.

A Song for Ukraine

I wanted to write a song for Ukraine,
But I gave up almost straight away.
An expert was required, ideally
Someone who would burrow into corners;
Go beneath the surface to smell the soil,
Who would press fighting flesh and procreate
And clasp lost strangers to their belly's bulge.
But how could I find a person like this?
Advertising? Perhaps. But in real life,
I knew I had to head toward the hills,
And to wait by that unbeatable view
For somebody sitting and reciting
From the pain of a life already done,
And staring, defiant, into madness.

Remorse

Crying like a baby,
The soldier sits alone.
He once thought his courage
Was chiselled into stone.

Although he has no fear
And ample will to fight,
He has no heart to kill;
He knows it is not right.

Beside him lies the corpse
That would have left him dead.
His instinct was to live
And shoot right through the head.

Yet, when the bullet struck
And this foe was no more,
He felt a twinge of pain,
Of life changed from before.

The soldier felt the ground,
Unsteady 'neath his feet.
He watched the light withdraw
From darkness in the street,

And watched the film replayed
Of his guilt and remorse.
Unarmed this time, he waits
For war to take its course.

Mykolaiv Zoo

(The zoo in Mykolaiv, a haven of calm close to the Eastern front, continues to care for its animals and to receive visitors, despite regular bombardments).

Species from all around the globe:
An elephant, a polar bear,
And here, an unexploded bomb.
Hang about, what's that doing there?

A tranquil spot during the week;
The animals make not a sound.
But the tail end of a rocket,
Protruding coldly from the ground,

Reveals the darker side to truth,
As locals pass with bike and pram.
An enemy would like us dead;
Tranquillity becomes a sham.

Refugee

I have nowhere to go,
Yet so much I could say;
No one out there listens
As my words fly away.

I have nowhere to sleep,
To lie down undisturbed.
My nightmares will run deep;
My tender dreams are curbed.

I have nowhere to hide,
No place where I can run.
I'll sit and contemplate
The cold, descending sun.

I have nowhere to grow,
And find out who I am.
My progress is too slow;
My future is a sham.

I have nowhere to mourn,
And yet I still can love.
My sweetheart's cherished soul
Floats ardent up above.

I have nowhere to die;
I knew that you would ask.
The dark, enclosing sky
Will carry out this task.